OHSAS 18001 Step by Step

A Practical Guide

OHSAS 18001
Step by Step

A Practical Guide

NAEEM SADIQ

IT Governance Publishing

IT Governance Publishing
IT Governance Limited
Unit 3, Clive Court
Bartholomew's Walk
Cambridgeshire Business Park
Ely
Cambridgeshire
CB7 4EA
United Kingdom

www.itgovernance.co.uk

First published in the United Kingdom in 2012 by IT Governance Publishing.

ISBN 978-1-84928-362-5

FOREWORD

People do not go to work in order to get injured or fall sick. 'Take care' and 'be safe' are often the last words exchanged with one's family before leaving home for work each day. It is, therefore, surprising that it took decades of indifference for organisations across the globe to realise that safe and healthy work environments are just about the first need of every individual who leaves home for work.

This book is about establishing an occupational health and safety (OH&S) management system based on the OHSAS 18001 standard. Occupational health deals with the promotion and maintenance of physical and mental health of workers, and their protection from disease and health-related risks. Safety, on the other hand, is often defined as freedom from unacceptable risk or harm. The subject of occupational health and safety, therefore, focuses on identification of health, as well as safety-related hazards, assessment of risks, and application of controls to eliminate, or minimise, the risks.

Driven by moral, legal and economic considerations, health and safety at work has come to play a vital role for individuals, as well as employers. It is both a moral and a legal obligation on the part of the management of a company to provide suitable conditions for work, and to exercise due diligence to prevent injury or ill health of all persons at work.

This pocket guide is for all those who wish to develop and implement an effective occupational health and safety (OH&S) management system based on OHSAS 18001. Standards often carry a formality about them, with each word bearing a specific meaning and context. They define requirements on 'what' must be done, without prescribing any specific details or methodology on 'how' it may be accomplished. This pocket guide is, therefore, an attempt to demystify the OHSAS 18001 standard, by presenting its contents and implementation methodology in a simple, user-friendly and easily understandable manner.

Foreword

This guide is ideal for managers, auditors, trainers and OH&S professionals who are involved in any aspect of an OHSAS 18001-based management system – may it be its development, implementation, training or auditing. The guide follows a hands-on and step-by-step approach. It explains the purpose and the requirements of each clause, and goes on to describe how these requirements may be fulfilled by an organisation. It includes numerous examples, suggestions, sample formats and sample procedures, to facilitate understanding and implementation, even by those individuals who may not have a previous background to this subject.

ABOUT THE AUTHOR

Naeem Sadiq holds a BS in Aerospace and a Masters degree in Manufacturing Engineering. Naeem is a certified lead auditor and lead trainer for ISO9001, OHSAS 18001 and ISO14001 standards. He is also an ASQ certified Manager and Quality System Auditor.

His work experience in engineering and management includes 16 years of working as an independent consultant, auditor, and trainer for ISO9001, OHSAS 18001 and ISO14001 standards.

Naeem has presented a number of papers in national conferences on management system standards, and has provided consultancy, training and auditing support to over 100 organisations. As a freelance writer, he is a regular contributor to national newspapers on safety, environment and social issues.

ACKNOWLEDGEMENTS

To all those individuals and organisations with whom I had the opportunity to interact as a friend, trainer, consultant or auditor, and who not only shared their experiences, but also asked hundreds of questions, whose answers I was compelled to seek.

To Asif Hayat, for sharing his ideas and materials from our earlier book – *ISO14001 Step by Step*, that we co-authored.

To Shifa, my wife, for her support, encouragement and proofreading, that goes far beyond this pocket guide.

I would like to thank the following for their helpful feedback when reviewing the manuscript: Chris Evans DPSM MBCS, ir H.L. (Maarten) Souw RE IT-Auditor, UWV and Antonio Velasco, CEO, Sinersys Technologies.

DISCLAIMER

All names, examples and values quoted in this book are fictitious and have been presented for learning, understanding and explaining purposes only.

Websites quoted in this pocket guide may change over a period of time, and the users may need to look up the new addresses where a change may have taken place.

CONTENTS

Contents

CHAPTER 1: WHAT IS OHSAS 18001?

OHSAS (Occupational Health and Safety Assessment Series) 18000 is an international occupational health and safety management system specification. OHSAS comprises of two parts, 18001 and 18002, and embraces a number of other publications. It is intended to help an organisation to control and manage its occupational health and safety risks.

OHSAS 18001 was jointly developed by a number of world-leading national standards bodies, certification bodies and specialist organisations, in response to a widespread demand for a recognised assessment and certification standard.

Like most other management system standards, OHSAS 18001 is designed on the principle of the Plan-Do-Check-Improve (PDCI) cycle. Planning for hazard identification, risk assessment and determination of controls, is a core requirement of an OH&S system. The standard makes it clear that the requirements of occupational health and safety apply to all activities, and all personnel who work for, or on behalf of, the organisation.

CHAPTER 2: OH&S MANAGEMENT SYSTEM GENERAL REQUIREMENTS (CLAUSE 4.1)

Clause 4.1 of OHSAS 18001 follows an approach which is consistent with most other management system standards, such as ISO9001 and ISO14001. It begins by making a comprehensive statement for establishing, documenting, implementing, maintaining and continually improving a management system, based on all the requirements stated in Clause 4 of OHSAS 18001.

These requirements are mandatory for any organisation that wants to control its OH&S risks and improve its OH&S performance. The standard follows the classic PDCI approach (establish, document, implement, maintain and improve), and unlike many other standards, it has no clauses on which an organisation may seek an exemption.

An organisation could be any company, corporation or enterprise, regardless of its size, which has its own functions and administration.

CHAPTER 3: OCCUPATIONAL HEALTH AND SAFETY POLICY (CLAUSE 4.2)

The OH&S policy is a statement that describes the overall intention, vision and direction of an organisation, relating to its OH&S performance. It is formally expressed by the organisation's top management, to reflect its commitment to protect health and safety of all personnel, to comply with all applicable laws, and to continually improve the OH&S performance of the organisation.

Summary of requirements

Establish an OH&S policy that includes:

1   Top management's commitment to prevention of injury and ill health, as well as continual improvement of its OH&S performance.
2   Commitment to comply with all regulatory and other applicable OH&S requirements.
3   A basis for setting OH&S objectives.

The OH&S policy must be approved, documented, periodically reviewed, and made available to all interested parties. (The intention here is to ensure that individuals are aware of their OH&S obligations.)

How can these requirements be met by an organisation?

Putting together an OH&S policy is essentially the responsibility of top management, who must take the following steps in order to meet the requirements of this clause of the standard:

1   Identify the nature and scale of hazards and risks that are associated with the organisation's occupational activities.
2   Define, document and approve an occupational health and safety policy that reflects top management's vision and commitment for prevention of injury and ill health.

Within the OH&S policy, top management must also state their commitment to comply with all applicable regulatory OH&S requirements, as well as a commitment to continually improve the organisation's OH&S performance. This could be done by describing the parameters, or the direction along which the continual improvement of OH&S performance is visualised. These directions can also become the basis for setting, and reviewing, an organisation's OH&S objectives.

3   Communicate the OH&S policy (after approval by top management) to all individuals within the organisation, along with their OH&S roles and responsibilities. An organisation could choose many methods to communicate its OH&S policy. These could include training sessions on policies and procedures, video messages, posters displayed at prominent locations, ongoing briefings, newsletters, e-mails, etc. The organisation must ensure that the language used for communicating its OH&S policy and procedures is easily understandable by all personnel.

4   Having defined and communicated its OH&S policy, the organisation must periodically review the policy for suitability and effectiveness. 'Management review' is one such platform which is normally used for review of OH&S policy. The frequency of review is a decision that must be made by an organisation itself.

An example occupational health and safety policy of Safe & Sound Inc. (SSI)

SSI believes in caring for the health and safety of all its employees, as well as other personnel who work for, or on behalf of, SSI. We commit to proactively work towards:

- Assessing the occupational health and safety risks, and to take steps to prevent injury and ill health to all personnel.

- Ensuring compliance to all applicable occupational health and safety regulatory requirements, as well as any other requirement to which SSI subscribes.

- Continually improving our OH&S management system, by setting and achieving higher performance goals. This shall include the reduction of OH&S incidents, providing a healthy work environment and moving towards becoming a zero injury organisation.

Chief Executive
Safe & Sound Inc.
Dated: 1April 2012 ver. 1

CHAPTER 4: HAZARD IDENTIFICATION, RISK ASSESSMENT AND DETERMINATION OF CONTROLS (CLAUSE 4.3.1)

Summary of requirements

Clause 4.3.1 of OHSAS 18001 requires the proactive assessment of hazards, risks and controls. This requirement is, therefore, central to the establishment of a sound OH&S system.

- An organisation is required to establish, and implement, procedures for ongoing hazard identification, risk assessment and determination of controls.

- Hazard identification must include infrastructure, equipment, human behaviours, capabilities, and routine and non-routine activities of all personnel.

- The risk assessment must consider applicable legal obligations and determine the risks that may be considered unacceptable to the organisation.

- The organisation must also determine controls to eliminate, substitute, or reduce the risks that have been assessed as intolerable.

- The identified OH&S hazards, risks and controls must be recorded, and taken into account while establishing an OH&S management system.

How can these requirements be met by an organisation?

1 Begin by establishing a cross-functional OH&S hazard identification and risk assessment team. The team members must be familiar with occupational health and safety issues, organisational processes, hazardous materials and conditions, applicable OH&S laws, human behaviour, human factors, types of OH&S hazards, risk assessment techniques and hierarchy of controls.

2 Document a procedure that defines the complete initial and ongoing process for identification of hazards, assessment of risks and determination of controls. *A sample procedure can be found in Appendix A.*

3 Make an inventory of all locations of the organisation, in such a manner that no department or area is missed out.

4 The cross-functional team visits each location and identifies both existing and potential hazards relating to a situation, source, activity or event that could potentially cause injury or ill health.

   o Hazardous situations are those conditions that are typical to a location and may cause injury or ill health. These could be slippery or uneven walking surfaces, slopes, cramped working conditions, sharp bends, blind corners, badly ventilated areas, high altitudes, extreme temperatures, high traffic zones, noisy locations, poorly lit areas or confined spaces.

   o Hazardous sources may be any equipment, or substances, that can cause injury or ill health. Some examples are production machines, generators, boilers, sources of fumes, corrosive and toxic chemicals, dangerous gases and liquids, flammable and explosive materials, high-pressure vessels, radioactive substances, particulates, poisons, bacteria and viruses.

   o The activity (routine or non-routine) -related OH&S hazards are those hazards that are faced by a person while performing a specific task. An operator working on a machine, welding a piece of metal, climbing on a height, lifting weight, handling or transferring materials, mixing chemicals, performing repetitive tasks and driving a vehicle, are some examples of activities that may offer one or more types of hazards.

   o Hazardous events, sometimes also referred to as emergency situations, are those events that may occur as a result of a failure, or absence of a control, and may cause injury or ill health. Some examples of such potentially hazardous events include explosions, implosions, fire, collisions, poisonous gas leaks, collapse of structures, road or aircraft accidents, and uncontrolled chemical reactions.

5   Hazard identification can be made easier by asking questions, such as:

- o Can a body part get caught in, or between, the objects?
- o Do tools, machines or equipment present any hazards?
- o Could the way an operator acts or behaves be a source of hazard?
- o Can the worker make harmful contact with moving objects?
- o Can the worker slip, trip or fall?
- o Can the worker suffer strain from lifting, pushing or pulling?
- o Is the worker exposed to extreme heat or cold?
- o Is there a possibility of electrical shock or electrocution?
- o Is the worker exposed to excessive noise or vibration?
- o Is there a danger from falling objects?
- o Can weather conditions affect safety?
- o Is harmful radiation a possibility?
- o Can contact be made with hot, toxic or caustic substances?
- o Are there dusts, fumes, mists or vapours in the air?
- o A list of potential occupational health and safety hazards can be found in Appendix C.

6   Once the hazards have been identified, the next step is to determine the 'risk' value for each identified hazard. Risk rating (R) is essentially a function of 'Likelihood' of occurrence (L), extent of 'Exposure' (E) and 'Severity' of outcome (S). All three factors collectively represent the 'risk' magnitude. Often organisations consider only 'Likelihood' and 'Severity' for estimating the risk value.

In such cases the 'Exposure' factor must be included in the estimation of 'Likelihood'. Considering the 'Likelihood' of occurrence of an event and the 'Severity' of harm that may be caused as a result of the occurrence, the Risk (R) may be calculated by using the simple formula $R = L \times S$. In order to achieve consistency in risk assessment, it is necessary to define a scale for various levels of likelihood and severity. (See sample procedure in Appendix A.)

Depending upon the activity and the nature of hazards and risks, an organisation may choose one of the many risk assessment techniques, such as Task Hazard Analysis (THA), Process Hazard Analysis (PHA), Hazard and Operability Study (HAZOP), What-if study, Failure Modes and Effects Analysis (FMEA), etc.

7   Risks can be better understood and managed if we consider all three stages of risk reduction, i.e. base risk, existing risk and final risk.

Base risk is the inherent risk of a source, situation or activity if there were no controls applied, or if the existing controls were to fail, decay or disappear for any reason (one typical reason could be an absence of a monitoring and inspection system). Hazards having a high base risk must be given due weightage while establishing and implementing an OH&S system, as their 'controls' are required to be constantly monitored and maintained.

The existing risk is the risk rating of a specific hazard at the time of carrying out the risk assessment, and takes into account all available and actively implemented controls. It is necessary for an organisation to assess if an existing risk must be tolerated, or whether additional measures should be taken to further minimise the risk. This would depend upon many factors, such as the level of an organisation's commitment towards prevention of injury and ill health, regulatory requirements, and the views of the interested parties. While organisations must attempt to reduce any risk to 'As Low As

Reasonably Possible' (ALARP) level, those which are above the 'tolerable level' (defined by the organisation) must be addressed without undue delay.

8   If the existing risk is beyond the tolerable level, it would become necessary to apply additional control measures to reduce the risk to an acceptable level. The recommended strategy for selection of additional controls is to begin with measures that would completely eliminate the hazard. If high noise is identified as a hazard, the first option should be to get rid of the source of the noise, rather than going for the ear plugs. There would be no need for further actions, if one could simply get rid of the source of the hazard.

The next best control is to substitute the hazardous substance or activity with a less hazardous one. Replacing a hazardous chemical with a less dangerous one; replacing oil-based paints with water-based paints; or replacing 40kg bags with lighter ones to reduce back and shoulder injuries, would be some examples of 'control' through substitution.

The next option should be to consider engineering controls. These are measures, such as electrical cut-out switches, pressure relief valves, barriers, machine guards, exhaust fans for ventilation, alarms, jammers, safety trips, interlocks, etc.

Next in the order of reliability are the administrative controls, such as establishing policies, procedures, labels, warning signs or training. These are designed to inform, or educate, workers of potential hazards, as well as to give instructions on dos and don'ts. Job rotation to reduce workers' exposure to a risk also falls in this category.

Personal protective equipment (PPE) is normally the last option. These are also the precautions that ought to be taken over and above the first four types of controls. PPE does not prevent an accident from happening, but could diminish the impact or severity in case it does happen. Hard hats, ear plugs, masks, safety shoes, gloves, aprons and safety belts are some of the more commonly used PPE.

9 Once the additional controls have been determined and implemented, the resultant risk (final risk) must be assessed, to confirm if the risk has actually been reduced to an acceptable level.

10 The risk assessment must be documented in a manner that describes the hazards identified, the risks assessed and the controls determined. *Appendix B describes one such format for a hazard and risk register.* The hazard and risk inventory is required to be kept constantly updated, as new hazards are identified. Establishing a simple hazard reporting system and encouraging employees to report hazards can be a very powerful tool to identify hazards on an ongoing basis.

11 The hazards, risks and controls thus determined must be taken into consideration while establishing and implementing an OH&S management system. Hazards, risks and controls provide key inputs into processes, such as objective setting, training needs analysis, measurement and monitoring, roles and responsibilities, audits, emergency planning, communication and consultation, operational controls and management reviews.

12 The process of hazard identification, risk assessment and determination of controls must also be applied prior to changes in existing equipment, installations, processes or procedures. The new designs, operations or equipment, must also undergo a risk assessment process during the early stages of design and installation. These activities must be covered by a documented procedure, often termed as MOC or a 'Management of Change' procedure.

CHAPTER 5: LEGAL AND OTHER REQUIREMENTS (CLAUSE 4.3.2)

Summary of requirements

- Establish and implement a procedure that defines how an organisation identifies and accesses the applicable legal and other OH&S requirements to which it subscribes.

- The requirements thus identified ought to be considered, while establishing and implementing the occupational health and safety management system.

- Finally, it is required that these requirements be kept updated and also communicated to the relevant interested parties.

How can these requirements be met by an organisation?

1 The first step in managing compliance with OH&S legal requirements is to know which requirements are applicable to an organisation. Each country has its own laws and regulatory requirements and hence it is mandatory for an organisation to identify the specific OH&S laws that it must be compliant with.

2 Planning for this subject must include a procedure that defines the mechanism of how an organisation identifies and obtains the applicable OH&S regulatory requirements. This information can normally be obtained from sources, such as government departments, ministries, websites, groups or organisations that originate or provide these laws. It is important that the organisation is able to access these sources on an ongoing basis, in order to keep itself abreast of the latest regulatory and other applicable requirements.

3 OHSAS 18001 requires that the applicable regulatory requirements are communicated to all concerned employees, as well as other interested parties, such as contractors, visitors, suppliers, etc.

4   An organisation can demonstrate compliance to Clause 4.3.2 of the OHSAS 18001 standard by taking the following three actions:

   o   Preparing, and keeping updated, a list of all sources and their names and addresses which are accessed by the organisation, to obtain latest OH&S regulatory requirements.

   o   Preparing and keeping updated a list of all applicable OH&S legislation and other requirements to which it subscribes.

   o   Disseminating the applicable requirements to all concerned persons mentioned above.

5   Some of the websites that could provide useful regulatory information about applicable OH&S regulations in Europe, UK, US, Germany, Japan, China, Canada and Australia, are given below.

Europe

- *www.iosh.co.uk/networks/international/international_links/europe.aspx*

UK

- Health and Safety at Work Act 1974 (*www.hse.gov.uk/legislation/hswa.htm*)
- A Guide to Health and Safety Regulation in Great Britain (*www.hse.gov.uk/pubns/web42.pdf*)

US

- Occupational Safety and Health Act US (*www.osha.gov/pls/oshaweb/owasrch.search_form?p_doc_type=oshact*)

Germany

- German Occupational Safety and Health Act (*http://osha.europa.eu//fop/germany/de/docs/legislation/ arbeitsschutzgesetz_englisch.pdf*)

Canada

- Canadian Occupational Health and Safety Regulations (*http://laws.justice.gc.ca/eng/regulations/SOR-86-304/index.html*)

Australia

- Australia OH&S Acts, Regulations and Codes (*www.weblaw.edu.au/display_page.phtml?WebLaw_Page=Occupational+Health+%26+Safety+Law*)
- *www.comcare.gov.au/laws__and__regulations/ohs_act,_ regulations__and__code*

China

- Workplace Safety and Health Act (*www.mom.gov.sg/legislation/occupational-safety-health/Pages/workplace-safety-health-act.aspx*)

Japan

- *www.jniosh.go.jp/icpro/jicosh-old/english/law/index.html*

Records to be kept

- An updated list of all sources that are accessed for obtaining OH&S regulatory requirements.
- An updated list of all applicable OH&S legislation and other requirements to which an organisation subscribes.

CHAPTER 6: OBJECTIVES AND PROGRAMME(S)
(CLAUSE 4.3.3)

Summary of requirements

- An organisation is required to establish documented and measurable OH&S objectives for relevant functions within the organisation.

- These objectives should be consistent with OH&S policy, including management's commitment to prevention of injury and ill health, compliance with laws, OH&S risks and commitment to continual improvement.

- Once the objectives have been established, the organisation must prepare plans that define responsibilities, resources and time-frames to achieve these objectives. Plans should be reviewed at regular intervals, to ensure that the organisation is able to achieve its defined objectives.

How can these requirements be met by an organisation?

1 Consider the following factors whilst setting OH&S objectives and targets:
   o OH&S policy is the basic input for an organisation's 'objective' setting process, as it states top management's commitment for prevention of ill health and injury, as well as continual improvement of OH&S performance.
   o The next important consideration should be the significant hazards and risks, as well as the regulatory requirements to which an organisation subscribes.
   o Objective setting should also consider the views and concerns of different stakeholders on matters of health and safety.
   o Technological, financial, operational and business considerations could also dictate decisions and priorities in establishing OH&S objectives.

2   *A few examples of OH&S objectives are given in Figure 1 below.*

1.	Improving the health of employees by reducing the number of asthma-related cases. This shall be achieved by aiming to reduce at least 50% of cases of asthma by June 2013. These shall be measured against the number of similar cases reported in 2011.
2.	We shall proactively improve the OH&S performance by creating an incentive scheme to motivate employees to report potential hazards. Starting in June 2012, each individual shall report at least two hazards per month, relating to his/her workplace.
3.	By June 2013, the noise level in the production hall shall be reduced from 90dB to 80dB, and in the generator room, from 85dB to75 dB.
4.	To reduce, by December 2012, the number of incidents of machine-related cuts and injuries on the foil wrapping machine, by at least 50% of the incidents reported in 2011.

Figure 1: Some examples of OH&S objectives

3   Needless to say, an organisation shall have only a small chance of achieving its OH&S objectives unless they are backed up by well-defined plans, resources, responsibilities and milestones. Hence the need for establishing plans that define the way forward for achieving an organisation's OH&S objectives. *An example of one such OH&S programme is given in Figure 2.*

OBJECTIVE: To reduce, by December 2012, the number of incidents of machine-related cuts and injuries on the foil wrapping machine, by at least 50% of the incidents reported in 2011.

Se. No	Actions/projects	Responsibility	Target date
1	Release of funds for machine door interlocks and training of personnel.	Manager Finance	March 2012
2	Select and install the machine door safety interlocks that immediately stop the machines, in case the door is opened for any reason.	Manager Engineering	May 2012
3	Training of operators on safe practices, especially switching off the machines before making any adjustments.	Engineering Manager	April 2012
4	Introducing an improved preventive maintenance system that enhances machine reliability and reduces the need of operators to frequently make machine	Engineering Manager	June 2012

	adjustments.		
5	Implementing a 'permit to work' system that includes lock out and tag out before any maintenance activity is undertaken.	Manager Maintenance	July 2012

Figure 2: Example of an OH&S programme

4 Monitor the extent to which the OH&S objectives and targets are being met. These must be monitored along the timelines established in OH&S programmes. This can be done by defining a frequency at which the OH&S management programmes must be reviewed, and where required, adjusted, to ensure timely achievement of the defined objectives. The information relating to the achievement of OH&S objectives should be provided to top management for review of OH&S performance. Top management could use this information to ascertain whether:

o   The OH&S objectives and targets are being achieved as planned.
o   There is a need for additional resources.
o   There is a need to modify the planned objectives, targets and programmes.
o   The OH&S objectives are effective in improving the OH&S performance of the company.

CHAPTER 7: RESOURCES, ROLES, RESPONSIBILITY, ACCOUNTABILITY AND AUTHORITY (CLAUSE 4.4.1)

Summary of requirements

- The ultimate responsibility for OH&S rests with the chief executive.

- Top management shall provide resources to implement and improve the OH&S system.

- Top management shall define, delegate, document and communicate OH&S roles and responsibilities.

- A member of top management is appointed to ensure that the OH&S management system is established and implemented. They must also report about the system's performance to the top management.

- Ensure that personnel at all levels understand and perform their assigned OH&S roles and responsibilities.

How can these requirements be met by an organisation?

1 Identify all tasks and roles that are required to establish, implement and improve the OH&S management system. This could include tasks, such as identification of OH&S hazards, assessment of risks, determination of controls, establishment of OH&S objectives, ensuring application of identified controls, planning, measuring and monitoring of OH&S performance, training, auditing, establishing a document control system, communicating with internal and external bodies, and ensuring regulatory compliance, etc.

2 Nominate individuals, functions and teams who shall have the responsibility and authority to undertake the defined OH&S tasks. Also, define how various roles, individuals, committees and functions are linked to each other. This can be done by any means, such as an organisation chart, a relationship chart, a process flow chart, etc.

3   The next step is to ensure that the individuals are competent to perform their assigned roles. (*See Chapter 8 for competency requirements.*)

4   Top management must nominate a competent person as the 'management representative' for the OH&S management system. They must have the authority to ensure that OH&S is established, implemented and maintained according to the requirements of OHSAS 18001. They must also report OH&S management system performance to top management for review and further improvement. Appendix K shows a sample input report, prepared by a 'management representative', for review by top management.

5   Some aspects of a management representative's competence could include knowledge of occupational health and safety issues, knowledge of OHSAS 18000 standards, applicable regulatory requirements, hazard identification and risk assessment techniques, operational controls, document and record control, internal audits and good communication skills.

6   Information on the identity of the designated OH&S management representative should be communicated to all members of the organisation.

Records to be kept

- OH&S roles, responsibility and authority of individuals and teams at various levels of the organisation.

- Organisation/interrelationship chart, or description of the linkages between individuals and teams that perform various OH&S tasks.

CHAPTER 8: COMPETENCE, TRAINING AND AWARENESS (CLAUSE 4.4.2)

Summary of requirements

- All persons working for an organisation must be competent to perform their assigned OH&S roles.

- OH&S training needs shall be identified, and steps taken to enhance competence, where any gaps are identified. Training should consider the level of risk, literacy and the language skills of the trainees.

- Procedures shall be established to make personnel aware of their OH&S roles and responsibilities, consequences of their behaviour and activities, emergency preparedness and response, benefits of improved performance and potential harm of departure from procedures.

How can these requirements be met by an organisation?

The following step-by-step approach, backed up by a procedure, could effectively meet the requirements of this clause:

1 From the hazard and risk assessment already carried out, identify all those tasks which are associated with health or safety hazards. These should include routine and non-routine tasks, as well as those performed in emergency situations.

2 Determine what competence is required by an individual, or a team, to perform these identified tasks. This should include employees, as well as contractors and others who perform work on behalf of the organisation.

3 Competence must be determined by considering all factors that work together to enable an individual to perform an assigned task safely, correctly and effectively. These factors may be a combination of knowledge, skill, ability, experience and attitude. Figure 3 shows a sample of competence criteria for a boiler supervisor.

A person who holds a government approved boiler operator licence and has two years' practical experience of working on gas-fired boilers. He/she should have knowledge of hazard identification, risk assessment, boiler legislation, personal protective equipment and chemicals used in the boiler house. He/she should have the ability to diagnose boiler defects, respond to boiler emergencies and carry out periodic maintenance of boilers. The person shall be required to act as a team leader for the boiler house team and take independent decisions to ensure that the boiler operates safely.

Figure 3: A sample of competence criteria for a boiler supervisor

4   The skills, knowledge and competence of the staff should be periodically checked against the defined requirements (competence criteria). Actions should be taken to fill the identified gaps.

5   It is important to verify if the training or skills provided were effective, and did in fact result in achieving the intended results. Effectiveness may be determined by using any one or more evaluation methods, such as feedback from the trainees, ongoing tests, end of the course examination and/or practical testing for skill-based subjects.

6   *Appendix D shows a sample procedure for establishing an OH&S competence, training and awareness process in an organisation.*

Records to be kept

• Record of competence criteria for each task

• Record of periodic verification of competence

8: Competence, Training and Awareness
(Clause 4.4.2)

- Record of training needs analysis
- Training plan or training calendar
- Record of training provided, such as training results, training attendance sheets and certificates of training and education
- Records of training effectiveness.

CHAPTER 9: COMMUNICATION, PARTICIPATION AND CONSULTATION (CLAUSE 4.4.3)

Summary of requirements

An organisation must have procedure(s) on:

- How it communicates OH&S information among its employees, contractors and visitors.
- How OH&S information from external sources is received, documented and responded to.
- How the involvement of workers (to the extent it is appropriate) is ensured in processes, such as risk assessment, incident investigation and the development of new OH&S policies.
- How workers are represented and consulted on matters that affect their OH&S.
- How contractors and other interested parties are consulted on relevant OH&S issues.

How can these requirements be met by an organisation?

The following step-by-step approach, supported by a procedure, could effectively meet the requirements of this clause:

1 Define when, and what, OH&S information needs to be communicated to contractors and visitors. Designate an individual, to ensure that this function is performed on an ongoing basis.

2 OH&S information to visitors would usually include safety precautions to be taken, personal protective equipment to be worn, areas to be visited (or not visited) and actions to be taken in case of emergency, etc.

3 The organisation is responsible for the OH&S of contractors at the workplace, and thus an ongoing process of OH&S communication must be established between

the contractors and the organisation. Communication with contractors may be spread over many phases. These could be contractor evaluation stage, contract making stage, induction stage (briefings and trainings at the time of beginning the work), monitoring and auditing stage (while the work is in progress), and finally, the task completion stage, when the area, equipment or the infrastructure is handed back to the organisation in a safe condition. Information on the OH&S aspects of 'permit to work' and its constant monitoring are equally important components of communication between the contractor and the organisation.

4   There are many methods in which an organisation conducts internal OH&S communication between various individuals, functions and levels. While computers, the Internet and e-mails have greatly facilitated this process, other methods, such as the ones listed below, could also be used for ensuring that the communication is received and understood at all levels.

   o   Meetings at various levels of management and employees to discuss and review OH&S issues and concerns. Shop floor OH&S meetings, quality circle meetings, safety committee meetings and management review meetings, are some of the platforms used by organisations to communicate OH&S-related issues

   o   Newsletters

   o   Suggestion boxes

   o   Establishing a hazard and incident reporting process

   o   Training sessions

   o   Communicating documented procedures

   o   Display or bulletin boards to communicate OH&S instructions, objectives, procedures and policies

   o   One-on-one behaviour safety contacts

   o   Process of reporting OH&S performance to top management.

5   Designate an individual to receive, document and respond to all OH&S-related communication with external parties. These could be vendors, suppliers,

contractors, community, neighbours, groups working on OH&S issues, government departments and regulatory bodies.

6 Clause 4.4.3 also requires that a procedure be established that describes the processes adopted by an organisation for its internal and external communication. The procedure must also clarify the different platforms and arrangements that are available to workers to raise their OH&S concerns, or to participate in OH&S matters. The identity of workers' representative on matters relating to OH&S must also be communicated to all employees.

Records to be kept

Records that relate to communication, participation and consultation could include:

- Minutes of OH&S meetings held at various levels and functions.

- Records of receiving and responding to external OH&S-related communication.

- Nomination of workers' representative on OH&S matters.

- Record of communication with contractors and visitors.

- Record of workers' involvement in hazard reporting, incident investigation and development of OH&S policies.

CHAPTER 10: DOCUMENTATION AND CONTROL OF DOCUMENTS
(CLAUSE 4.4.4 AND 4.4.5)

Summary of requirements

1 The OH&S documentation should be as simple, minimum and efficient as possible. It should include the following:
   o OH&S scope, policy, objectives and targets.
   o Description of the main elements of the OH&S management system and their interaction.
   o Procedures and records required by OHSAS 18001 and those determined by the organisation for effective management of their own OH&S processes and risks.

2 An organisation is also required to establish a procedure that defines how it controls (approves, reviews, changes, identifies, disseminates and removes obsolete versions) documents of internal and external origin.

How can these requirements be met by an organisation?

It is best to explain the difference between the two often interchangeably used terms 'documents' and 'records', before proceeding to the main contents of this chapter.

Documents

Documents provide information, data, policies, procedures or instructions, and could use any medium, such as print or electronic. Some examples of documents are:

- Policies, objectives, targets, programmes, manuals, standard operating procedures, work instructions, process flow charts or plans.
- Photographs, videos, sketches or drawings providing instructions.

- Documents of external nature, such as regulatory requirements or international standards.
- Formats and checklists (when blank).

Records

Records are a special category of documents. They provide evidence, facts or results of actions taken, or tasks performed by an organisation. Some examples of records are:

- Equipment maintenance and inspection records.
- Certification and licences obtained.
- Audit records, such as audit reports and observations.
- Minutes of meetings, such as safety committee meeting, management review meeting.
- Record of training need analysis, training conducted and training effectiveness.
- Record of calibration of measuring devices.
- Record of compliance with regulatory OH&S requirements.

Begin by preparing an OH&S core document, or a manual. This should include the following:

- The 'scope' of your organisation's OH&S management system. Typically, an OH&S management system's scope will include the core function/activities of the organisation and the location(s) at which these activities are performed.

An example of an organisation's OH&S management system scope could be:

'Safe and Sound Inc, located at 108 Esplanade Ave West, Building 310, North Vancouver is engaged in manufacture and sale of single and multi core electrical wires, rods and cables.'

- Description of the main elements of the OH&S management system and how they are interlinked to each other.

- Include, or give reference to, OH&S procedures and other supporting documents that are used in planning, implementing or controlling OH&S activities of the organisation.

Define a procedure that describes how an organisation controls its internal and external documents. The following elements of document control must be included in this procedure:

- Nominate a person to carry out the responsibility for control of OH&S documentation.

- List all internal and external documents that are used in the OH&S management system.

- Describe the review and approval authority for each OH&S document, and ensure all controlled documents are approved by the appropriate authorised persons.

- Define a document numbering system, so that each OH&S document bears a unique number, such as S&S-Procedure-23 or S&S- SOP-12.

- Mention the latest revision status and date on each OH&S document, such as Rev.3 dated 10.3.2012.

- Identify the individuals or locations that ought to receive relevant documentation, and ensure that they receive the latest version of applicable documents.

- The procedure must define how obsolete documents are removed, prevented from unintended use and replaced by latest versions.

- Maintaining an updated list that includes names, reference numbers, revision dates, revision levels, and distribution of all internal and external documents, is an effective way to establish control over OH&S management system documents.

10: Documentation and Control of Documents (Clause 4.4.4 and 4.4.5)

Appendix E describes the documents and procedures required by OHSAS 18001.

CHAPTER 11: OPERATIONAL CONTROLS (CLAUSE 4.4.6)

Summary of requirements

- Identify operations and activities which are associated with hazards, and where controls must be applied to minimise hazards and manage OH&S risks.
- Operational controls include documented procedures and operating criteria for the safe functioning of processes, activities and equipment.
- OH&S controls must also be implemented over contractors, visitors, purchased goods, equipment and services.

How can these requirements be met by an organisation?

Operational controls may be defined as all those measures, methods and precautions taken to manage OH&S risks of an organisation's activities and operations. The organisation must plan these activities to ensure that they are carried out under controlled conditions. These conditions (including operating criteria) must be specified in documented procedures, especially for situations where their absence could lead to deviations from the OH&S policy, procedures or objectives.

While all controls identified in the risk assessment need to be addressed, following are some of those activities, situations or sources that would require application of documented controls to manage risks:

- Operations relating to critical pressure equipment.
- Operations involving substances, such as flammable liquids, hazardous gases, ammonia, enzymes, acids, hazardous chemicals, etc.
- Working at heights.
- Working with high voltage or other energy sources.

- Operation of fork-lift trucks, cranes, lifts and heavy lifting equipment.
- Hot work and electric arc welding.
- Controls for safe driving of vehicles.
- Controls over suppliers, vendors and visitors.
- Machinery, equipment and materials which can cause harm, ill health or injury.
- Contractor management.
- Maintenance of plant and equipment.
- Noise, dust, light and ergonomic issues related to workplace operations.
- Handling and storage of hazardous chemicals and gases.
- Management of risks through 'permit to work' system.
- Management of change.

Three sample operational control procedures have been included in this pocket guide. These are:

- *A sample procedure for critical pressure equipment (Appendix F).*
- *A sample procedure for 'permit to work' (Appendix G).*
- *A sample procedure for fork-lift trucks (Appendix H).*

CHAPTER 12: EMERGENCY PREPAREDNESS AND RESPONSE (CLAUSE 4.4.7)

Summary of requirements

- Identify all possible OH&S emergency situations that may arise in an organisation.

- Plan, prepare and respond to emergency situations (to minimise harm to life and property) and also mitigate adverse consequences.

- Establish procedure(s) for emergency preparedness and response, and periodically test them to determine their effectiveness.

- Periodically review emergency procedures in the light of lessons learnt, either during emergency drills or from actual emergencies.

How can these requirements be met by an organisation?

The emergency planning process may bring to light deficiencies, such as lack of equipment or trained personnel. It could also highlight issues that can be corrected before the occurrence of an actual emergency (such as identifying an inoperative fire water pump). There are two main components of this clause, namely 'preparedness' and 'response'.

Preparedness

1   A good OH&S hazard identification and risk assessment of all routine and non-routine activities of an organisation should also result in identification of potential emergency situations. The organisation should make a list of all such potential OH&S emergency situations. These could be:
     o   Fire
     o   Explosion, implosion
     o   Accidental releases of toxic substances
     o   Work-related accidents, injuries, fatalities or other serious medical emergencies.

- o Natural disasters – lightning, earthquakes, floods, snow storms
- o Chemical spills
- o Crash, collision or structural collapse
- o Sabotage, vandalism, terrorist attack, bomb threat or riot.

2   The first priority should be to determine controls and measures that will ensure that the emergency situations do not occur (our approach should be preventive in nature).

3   As a next step, planning must be carried out to prepare an organisation to respond to an emergency situation if it still occurs, despite the controls implemented or precautions taken. These preparations shall involve persons, equipment, methods and tasks, such as:

- o Defining an emergency organisation, its functions and responsibilities. These could be responsibilities, such as declaration of emergency, assuming overall command, ordering evacuation, alerting external agencies, confirming successful evacuation, requesting external aid, providing medical help and sounding all-clear, etc.
- o Defining what equipment (vehicles, fire extinguishers, stretchers, ambulances, cranes, search lights, evacuation equipment, communication equipment, respirators, medical supplies, fire hydrants, fire vehicles, etc.) will be required for an effective emergency response. Ensuring that this equipment is identified, made available, periodically inspected and always kept in a ready state.
- o Defining contact numbers and addresses of all agencies and individuals who need to be contacted in case of an emergency. These could be individuals within the organisation, as well as outside agencies, such as hospitals, fire stations, emergency organisations, police stations, government agencies, etc.
- o Defining and preparing information and communication processes needed in an emergency.

These may include location maps, layout of electrical cabling and gas pipes, location of fire hydrants, assembly points, etc.

o Training individuals for their roles in emergency situations.

o Defining evacuation and assembly procedures, exit routes, assembly points, head-count methodology and other planned arrangements for emergency management. Clearly mark assembly points, as well as exit routes and doors. Give special consideration to how physically challenged persons will be evacuated in emergency situations.

o Identifying equipment that either prevents an emergency from taking place, or warns of an impending emergency. Such equipment could be alarms, trips, smoke detectors, pressure relief valves, cut-off relays or non-return valves. Prepare plans and carry out regular inspection and maintenance of all emergency equipment.

o Documenting the above processes in an emergency preparedness and response procedure.

Response

1 An effective response must aim to prevent fatalities and injuries, reduce damage to plant and equipment, contain the spread of damage and help in early resumption of normal operations.

2 In order to effectively respond to emergency situations, an organisation must rehearse its emergency plans by carrying out periodic rehearsals or drills. These rehearsals could help in identifying the following:

o Are the procedures adequate to effectively respond to situations of real emergencies and accidents?

o Do all persons understand their roles and know how to respond in situations of emergency? Are they well trained?

o Is the emergency response equipment maintained in good condition, and is it sufficient and effective for its intended functions?

3 An organisation must test its emergency plans by simulating its identified potential emergencies as close to real conditions as practicable. However, such drills would have a learning value only if they are closely monitored for accomplishment of their key performance indicators, e.g. response time, ability to contain a spill, effectiveness of fire fighting team, effectiveness and adequacy of emergency equipment, ability to evacuate in a timely manner, response of first aiders, timely arrival of ambulance, transfer to hospitals and effectiveness of mitigation measures. Results of such drills must be recorded and analysed for further improvement of the emergency response process.

4 Emergency procedures must be reviewed at planned intervals and also after the occurrence of an accident or an emergency. This is done to ensure continuing adequacy and suitability of the emergency preparedness and response procedures.

Records to be kept

- Record of emergency drills and their effectiveness.
- Record of review of procedures and plans (where applicable) after conducting emergency drills or after real emergencies.
- Record of emergency equipment inspections.
- Record of training and awareness on various aspects of emergency preparedness and response.

CHAPTER 13: PERFORMANCE MEASUREMENT, MONITORING AND EVALUATION OF COMPLIANCE (CLAUSE 4.5.1 AND 4.5.2)

Summary of requirements

1 An organisation must establish and implement procedure(s) to monitor :
   o Its OH&S performance (using proactive and reactive measures)
   o The extent to which its OH&S objectives are met.

2 Equipment used for measurement and monitoring of OH&S performance must be calibrated.

3 The organisation must also periodically evaluate compliance with OH&S legal and other requirements to which it subscribes and keep a record of these periodic evaluations.

How can these requirements be met by an organisation?

OH&S performance can be termed as the effectiveness of all those measures that are implemented to prevent injury and disease to persons at the workplace. These measures could be arrangements for identifying hazards, assessing and controlling risks, monitoring and improving OH&S parameters or compliance against legal requirements. OH&S performance must be measured and monitored by proactive, as well as reactive, parameters. These parameters are also referred to as key performance indicators or KPIs. Good performance against proactive parameters should lead to good outcomes of reactive KPIs.

1 The proactive measures (or leading indicators) of performance are initiatives that would help in preventing workplace injury and illness. These could be:
   o Number of risk assessments completed.
   o Number of OH&S equipment inspections carried out.
   o Number of emergency drills conducted.

- o Number of 'walk-around' or 'deep compliance' inspections completed.
- o Number of 'behaviour safety' contacts made.
- o Extent to which OH&S objectives are met.
- o Number of 'defensive driving' trainings conducted.
- o Number of OH&S training and awareness sessions completed.
- o Number of near miss incidents reported.
- o Percentage of reported hazards rectified within the defined timeframe.
- o Number of supervisory inspections completed.
- o Number of safety committee meetings held.
- o Percentage of design changes made to address identified OH&S issues over the life of a project.
- o Number of internal OH&S management system audits completed.
- o Number of 'tool box talks' conducted during a defined period.
- o Number of proactive health or noise surveys.

2   The reactive measures (or lagging indicators) of OH&S performance relate to the outcomes of measurement and monitoring. While 'outcome' indicators are important, they generally reflect the results of past actions. It is also possible for outcome indicators to hide potential risks. For example, having a low incidence of injury does not necessarily mean that adequate safety systems and controls are in place. Reactive KPIs could be accidents, incidents, non-conformances or events that occurred in a given time period, such as:

- o Number of lost time accidents (LTAs)
- o Number of restricted work cases (RWCs)
- o Number of medical treatment cases (MTCs)
- o Number of fatalities
- o Vehicle collisions and injuries
- o Number of system-related non-conforming situations identified.

3   Monitor OH&S objectives against the time-frame defined in management programmes. These should be measured

on a regular basis and the progress reported to top management.

4   Compliance with applicable OH&S regulatory requirements (and other rules to which an organisation subscribes) is a mandatory requirement of clause 4.5.2 of the standard. This requirement can be met by an organisation by periodically (say once or twice every year) evaluating and confirming its compliance against all applicable requirements. This information is also an essential input to the management review process. The results of periodic evaluation of compliance must be retained as records.

5   It is normal for an organisation to use a number of instruments or measuring devices to measure and monitor its OH&S performance. These could be instruments, such as decibel meters, temperature or pressure gauges, volt meters, dosimeters, dust monitors, weighing scales, air flow meters, accelerometers, luxmeters, gas leak and emission detectors, etc. An organisation needs to ensure that a calibration system is established for calibration of such measuring instruments. The following simple steps could enable the implementation of an effective calibration process:

   o   Make a list of all OH&S measurement and monitoring equipment.
   o   Give a unique identification number to each equipment.
   o   Define the frequency of calibration for each equipment.
   o   At the defined frequency, calibrate the equipment against another equipment of known accuracy.
   o   Apply labels on every equipment for last date and next date of calibration.
   o   Maintain calibration records.

6   A measurement and monitoring plan should form the core of the OH&S measuring and monitoring process. A measurement and monitoring plan is often a summary of who, when and what is measured and monitored in an

organisation. It would include the following pieces of information:

o Proactive and reactive parameters (KPIs) to be measured/monitored.

o Responsibility for measurement, monitoring and analysis of each KPI.

o Procedures used for measurement, monitoring and review.

o Frequency of measurement or monitoring of KPIs.

o Process, responsibility and frequency for monitoring the extent to which OH&S objectives have been achieved.

o Process, responsibility and frequency for review of compliance with OH&S regulatory and other requirements.

o Process, responsibility and frequency for internal OH&S audits.

o Records to be kept.

CHAPTER 14: INCIDENT INVESTIGATION, NON-CONFORMITY, CORRECTIVE AND PREVENTIVE ACTION (CLAUSE 4.5.3)

Summary of requirements

- Establish a system to record, investigate and analyse incidents in a timely manner.
- Establish a system to take effective corrective and preventive actions for actual and potential non-conformities.
- Conduct a risk assessment prior to implementing corrective or preventive actions, if these actions involve new or changed hazards.
- Ensure changes are made in the OH&S documentation (where required) as a result of corrective and preventive actions.

How can these requirements be met by an organisation?

It may be best to explain, in simple words, the meaning of terms used in this chapter.

Incident: An incident is any work-related event that caused, or could have caused, injury or ill health, regardless of its severity.

Accident: An accident is a category of incident that actually resulted in injury or ill health, regardless of its severity.

Near miss: An incident that caused no ill health, injury or harm but came very close to doing so, is also termed as a near miss. While a near miss may have caused no harm, it is important to treat it with the same degree of importance (investigate and take preventive actions) as an accident.

Corrective actions: Correcting an existing non-conformity and eliminating its root cause, by taking actions that will avoid its recurrence.

Preventive actions: Eliminating the causes of a potential non-conformity, by taking actions that will prevent its occurrence.

Non-conformity: A non-conformity is any condition, act, document, product or process that does not comply with a requirement that may be defined by law, standards or an organisation's own policies, plans and procedures. A non-conformity may have already occurred (existing non-conformity) or may have the potential to occur (potential non-conformity).

An organisation may identify existing OH&S management system non-conformities by any of the following methods:

- While conducting an internal or external OH&S management system or a process specific OH&S audit.
- As a result of investigation into an OH&S incident.
- While measuring, monitoring, inspecting or testing for OH&S compliance.
- When an OH&S deviation is identified by a regulatory body, employee or any other interested party.

An organisation can create an effective OH&S incident reporting and investigation process by implementing the following steps:

- Defining an incident reporting system which encourages, and enables, all personnel to report incidents, even when no ill health or injury has been actually caused.
- Documenting and implementing a procedure that describes the process of reporting and conducting an investigation, roles and responsibilities of investigating team, guidelines for investigation, taking early corrective actions and recording the results of investigations.

Once an existing or potential OH&S non-conformity has been identified, the following steps must be implemented:

- Take immediate actions necessary to correct and mitigate the non-conforming situation. These may be replacing a safety relief valve, providing immediate medical treatment, extinguishing and curtailing a fire, putting a machine guard back in its place or providing training to an individual.

- Investigate and identify the root causes of the non-conformity. It is necessary to differentiate between immediate and root causes. Consider the example of an operator getting injured after falling from a roof. While falling from the roof describes the type of incident, absence of a railing could be its immediate cause. The root causes may be the absence of hazard identification and risk assessment, lack of management commitment or inadequate procedures for working at heights. Often there is more than one root cause that contributes to an incident, and these must all be investigated and addressed. Elimination of root causes is a common requirement for addressing the existing, as well as potential, non-conformities. It is appropriate that the person investigating the root causes is someone who is competent in the tools of root cause analysis, such as 'cause and effect diagram', 'why-why analysis', 'barrier analysis', 'fault tree analysis', 'failure mode and effect analysis', etc.

- For existing non-conformities, take actions to eliminate the root cause(s), so as to prevent recurrence of the non-conformity. This requires addressing the immediate causes, as well as the root causes. When handling potential non-conformities, take actions to eliminate the root cause(s), so as to prevent occurrence of the potential non-conformity.

- Verify actions taken for adequacy and effectiveness. Problems often re-occur if the corrective actions were inadequate or ineffective. The verification process is, therefore, a way of evaluating if all holes (root causes) have been plugged. Evaluating the effectiveness of corrective actions should include investigating all other areas, people, equipment and procedures for similar deficiencies.

- An organisation remains vulnerable to a hazardous situation until it has been controlled or eliminated. It is, therefore, important not to delay the investigation, and to take the corrective or preventive actions as early as possible.

Records to be kept

- Record of incidents reported
- Record of investigation of incidents
- Record of non-conformities identified. (*Appendix I shows a suggested format for a non-conformity report*)
- Record of corrective actions and review of their effectiveness
- Record of preventive actions and review of their effectiveness.

CHAPTER 15: CONTROL OF RECORDS (CLAUSE 4.5.4)

Summary of requirements

- Establish a system for creation and maintenance of records, to demonstrate conformity to OH&S requirements stated in OHSAS 18001 and those determined by the organisation itself.

- Create identification and traceability for OH&S records and store them in a manner that they are protected, as well as easily retrievable.

- Define the retention period for OH&S records and retain them for the stated period.

How can these requirements be met by an organisation?

Records demonstrate and provide evidence of the results achieved, and the activities performed as a requirement of OHSAS 18001, or the planned arrangements defined in an organisation's own OH&S management system. The process and activities of a record management system must be defined in a 'record control' procedure. These could be actions, such as:

- Defining and making a list of records to be maintained in order to demonstrate compliance to regulatory requirements, OHSAS 18001 and the requirements established by an organisation in its OH&S management system.

- Determining how records shall be identified. Data, such as name, number, date (when the record was made) and the person (who authorised the record), is often used to give a unique identification to a record.

- Defining a retention period for each record. This could be based on regulatory requirements, data analysis, audit or continual improvement considerations.

- Describing how and where the records will be stored. This is necessary to ensure protection, as well as easy retrievability of records.

Records can be easily controlled by listing them on a format, such as the one found in Appendix J.

CHAPTER 16: INTERNAL AUDIT
(CLAUSE 4.5.5)

Summary of requirements

- Establish an audit procedure that defines the responsibilities for planning, conducting, reporting and follow-up of internal OH&S management system audits.
- Conduct audits at intervals planned on the basis of significance of risks, as well as the results of previous audits.
- Determine if the OH&S management system conforms to the requirements of OHSAS 18001, and is effective in meeting its own objectives and planned arrangements.
- Select auditors who are objective and impartial.

How can these requirements be met by an organisation?

It is best to begin by seeking clarity on the meaning of terms used in the audit process. These are:

Audit: An audit is essentially a process of independently obtaining evidence, and evaluating it objectively, to determine the extent to which it meets a defined audit 'criteria'.

Audit criteria: Criteria represents a set of requirements against which an audit is carried out. The criteria for a complete OH&S internal audit would include requirements defined by OHSAS 18001, as well as applicable laws, policies, procedures and plans defined by an organisation's own OH&S management system.

Audit findings: Audit evidence when evaluated against audit criteria would result in either a conforming or a non-conforming situation. In both cases it would be termed as an 'audit finding'.

Implementing an internal OH&S audit process in an organisation requires the following steps:

- Begin by establishing an internal OH&S audit procedure.

- Nominate a competent person to assume overall responsibility for ensuring the tasks involved in audit planning, conducting, reporting and follow-up audits are implemented effectively.

- Prepare an audit plan which reflects the frequency, and the scope, of each audit. The audit plan must give due consideration to the significant hazards and risks of the organisation, and the results of the previous audits.

- Select and train a team of auditors for conducting OH&S management system audits. The competence of auditors plays an important role in the quality of audits, and therefore, it would be worthwhile to invest in auditor training and competence. A good OH&S auditor training programme could be spread over three to five days and include topics, such as principles of OH&S, hazard identification, risk assessment, hierarchy of controls, OH&S regulatory requirements, corrective and preventive actions, requirements of OHSAS 18001, audit guidelines mentioned in ISO19011, communication and knowledge of planning, conducting and reporting an audit.

- Share the audit plan with the auditors and the auditees. Auditors must prepare themselves by gaining awareness about specific hazards, risks, controls, processes, laws and documentation of the organisation, before the start of the audit. Preparation of audit checklists can be of great help in maintaining focus, managing audit time and ensuring that all requirements have been covered.

An auditor should collect evidence to determine the following:

- The extent to which an organisation complies with the requirements defined in OHSAS 18001.

- The extent to which the OH&S management system enables an organisation to meet its occupational health and safety objectives and planned arrangements. Planned arrangements include company policies, procedures and controls.

- The extent to which the OH&S management system enables an organisation to prevent, or minimise, occupational health and safety risks.

- The extent to which the OH&S management system enables an organisation to comply with regulatory, and other requirements, to which it subscribes.

- Is the OH&S management system implemented effectively and continually improved?

The independence of auditors is a mandatory requirement and can be ensured by not nominating an auditor for an activity that falls under his/her own area of responsibility. As an example, a manager responsible for implementation of 'permit to work' should not be asked to audit activities which are primarily controlled by a PTW system.

While raising non-conformities, auditors must always describe the evidence collected, and the specific clause of the standard, or the procedure, that was violated.

A critical skill of an auditor is his/her ability to verify the effectiveness of corrective actions. This must include considerations, such as:

- Was the identified non-conformity adequately mitigated and corrected?

- Was the root cause(s) identified correctly?

- Will the actions taken ensure that the root causes are eliminated and the non-conformity will not re-occur?

- Have other similar situations, activities, materials, locations and equipment, also been reviewed for removal of the same, or similar, non-conformance? A non-conformity is like a bad fish in a pond. Removing some and not others, will surely spoil the remaining fish in due course of time.

- Have the issues of shortcomings in training, organisational structure, adequacy of resources and management commitment been considered and addressed?

Records to be kept

- Audit plans
- Auditors' training and competence records
- Audit findings
- Audit reports, containing results of the audit
- Audit-related corrective actions and verification of their effectiveness.

CHAPTER 17: MANAGEMENT REVIEW (CLAUSE 4.6)

Summary of requirements

- It is the responsibility of the top management of an organisation to review the performance of its OH&S management system at defined intervals.

- The review must evaluate the performance and effectiveness of the OH&S management system, and explore possibilities for its further improvement.

- The review must be based on inputs, such as audit results, legal compliance, results of consultation with employees, communication with interested parties, achievement of objectives, corrective and preventive actions and recommendations for improvement.

- Top management should provide specific decisions and actions relating to continual improvements of its OH&S management system.

How can these requirements be met by an organisation?

'Management review' is the final, and the highest platform in an organisation, at which the performance and adequacy of the OH&S management system is reviewed. An organisation can take the following steps to establish an effective 'management review' process:

- Define the composition of the top management of the organisation. Normally, these are the senior most executives who have the ultimate responsibility for decisions and resources relating to the OH&S management system.

- Define the interval at which the OH&S management system shall be reviewed. Avoid too frequent (one to two months) or too infrequent reviews (more than 12 months).

- Create an effective measurement and monitoring system as a pre-requisite for a good 'management review'. It is this process (*described in Chapter 13*) that provides a complete picture of an organisation's OH&S performance to top management.

- Create an effective input report that includes all aspects of OH&S performance. It is the responsibility of the management representative of the OH&S management system (as required by clause 4.4.1b) to collect, collate and present this data as an input to the 'management review'. *A sample OH&S 'management review' input report is shown in Appendix K*. A 'management review' shall be just as good as the data or facts that are provided as an input to the process. Thus, a comprehensive input report containing specific facts and accurate results of the OH&S performance, can greatly improve the effectiveness of the 'management review' process.

- While reviewing the OH&S trends, top management should challenge the existing processes and push for continual improvement.

- Conclude the 'management review' by specific and time-bound decisions, with clearly defined responsibilities. These might relate either to correcting the existing deficiencies, or bringing further improvement in the OH&S management system performance.

Records to be kept

- Management review input report
- Records of management review that include issues discussed and decisions taken.

APPENDIX A: SAMPLE PROCEDURE FOR OH&S HAZARD IDENTIFICATION, RISK ASSESSMENT AND DETERMINATION OF CONTROLS

Purpose: To define a process that describes initial, and ongoing, identification of occupational health and safety hazards, assessment of risks and determination of controls.

Scope: This procedure is applicable to all locations, equipment, infrastructure and personnel (employees, contractors and visitors) who are involved in any routine or non-routine activity of Safe and Sound Inc. (SSI).

Responsibilities: Manager < > has the overall responsibility for the following activities:

- Formation of OH&S hazard and risk assessment teams, and ensuring their competence.
- Identification of hazards, assessment of risks and determination of controls (initial and ongoing).
- Maintenance and upkeep of OH&S hazard and risk register (*Appendix B*).

Procedure:

1   Make an inventory of all locations of the organisation, in such a manner that no area or department is missed out. SSI has been divided into 10 distinct locations and these are numbered as location 1 to location 10.

2   Nominate trained personnel to form cross-functional risk assessment teams for each location of SSI. Each cross-functional team shall visit its allocated location, identify the presence of hazards, and describe how the hazard may cause ill health, harm or injury. Ensure that every situation, source, activity or event that could potentially cause injury or ill health, is identified as a hazard. Ensure specialist advice is sought from a doctor (and where required, from a psychologist) on hazards and controls relating to health, such as hygiene, ergonomics, noise,

fumes, chemical reactions, human behaviour, capabilities and human factors. Use the following methods and sources for identification of hazards:

o Observations/examination
o Study of equipment and process flow diagrams
o Brainstorming and 'what-if analysis'
o Safety information from 'material safety data sheets'
o Data from previous incidents/accidents
o Medical records, first-aid cases and lost time accidents (LTAs)
o Views of interested parties (records of internal communication and participation)
o Legal and regulatory requirements.

3 Use the following rating/scale for assessment of likelihood and severity (needed for subsequent quantification of risk).

LIKELIHOOD (L) SCALE

Likelihood of occurrence
One in ... 10,000 chance 1
One in a 1,000 chance 2
One in a 100 chance 3
One in 50 chance.......................................4
One in 10 chance 5

SEVERITY (S) SCALE

The severity of harm
A minor scratch or first aid case.............1
Injury resulting in one–three days off
work...2
Injury resulting in more than
three days off work.................................3
Loss of limb/permanent disability..........4
One or more fatalities.............................5

4   Risk rating R is calculated by $R = L \times S$. Risk assessed as five or more would be considered intolerable, and would require mandatory application of additional controls in order to reduce the risk. The determination of controls must take into consideration the following top-down hierarchy.
   o   Elimination
   o   Substitution
   o   Engineering controls
   o   Administrative controls
   o   Personal protective equipment.

5   *Prepare a register of OH&S hazards, risks and controls for all locations of SSI, using the format in Appendix B.*

6   Review, and update, the register of OH&S hazards, risks and controls (*Appendix B*) at least once every year. Also, review and update whenever new hazards are identified, laws are changed, lessons are learnt from new incidents, or when processes and activities are added or modified.

Records to be kept

• Register of OH&S hazards, risks and controls

• Record of competence of the OH&S risk assessment team.

OH&S Hazard and Risk Register   Location:

Team members:

Situation, source, activity or event	Describe the hazard	Base risk BR=LxS			Controls already in place	Existing risk ER=LxS (Consider additional controls if risk rating => 5)			Additional controls determined	Final risk FR=LxS		
		L	S	R		L	S	R		L	S	R

APPENDIX C: TYPES OF OH&S HAZARDS

An OH&S hazard is any source, situation, activity or event that has the potential to cause injury or ill health, or both. The following is a list of typical potential hazards that could be found in a workplace:

- Ergonomic hazards, such as musculoskeletal disorders, carpal tunnel syndrome, tennis elbow, neck and back aches (normally due to over use of muscles, bad posture, repeated tasks, poorly designed workstations, lifting heavy weights, or tasks beyond an employee's physical capabilities and limitations).

- Hazards relating to dust, fumes and vapours.

- Biological hazards, such as bacteria, viruses, fungi, blood-borne pathogens, etc.

- Hazardous gases, such as carbon monoxide, ammonia, benzene, butane, chloroform, hydrogen sulphide, methane, etc.

- Chemical hazards of various categories, such as toxins, carcinogens, sensitisers, immunological agents, dermatopathic agents or asthmagens.

- Radiation hazards.

- Slips, trips, falls.

- Noise, vibration.

- Electricity and electrical hazards.

- Welding and hot work hazards.

- Asphyxiation.

- Cold stress (hypothermia).

- Confined space hazards.

- Falls from working at heights.

- Drugs, alcohol, tobacco.

- Heat stress, dehydration.

- Compressed air or high pressure fluids.
- Asbestos, lead, heavy metals, petroleum and silica hazards.
- Mechanical hazards (crushed fingers or hands, amputations, impact, collision, entanglement, crushing, cutting, shearing, abrasion, etc.).
- Hazards involved in driving, movement and operation of cranes, vehicles, forklifts and trolleys.
- Fire and explosion hazards.
- Hazards in office environment (stress, ergonomic hazards, temperature, humidity, light, noise, ventilation, space, task design, etc.).
- Psychosocial hazards could include work-related stress, excessive working hours (over time), violence, bullying, emotional or verbal abuse, sexual harassment, burn-out, etc.
- Hazardous substances, oils, perfumes, paints, acids, bases, enzymes, aerosols, etc.

APPENDIX D: SAMPLE PROCEDURE FOR TRAINING COMPETENCE AND AWARENESS

Purpose: To define responsibilities for planning, conducting and recording the process of OH&S training, competence and awareness, so that all personnel of Safe & Sound Inc. (SSI) are competent to safely perform their OH&S assignments.

Responsibilities: Manager < > has the overall responsibility to ensure that all personnel are competent for their relevant OH&S roles and responsibilities. They are also responsible for undertaking activities relating to need analysis, training provision and maintenance of OH&S training records.

Procedure:

1   Manager < >, in consultation with the concerned managers and experts of each department, shall be responsible to undertake the following activities:
    o   Prepare a list of all OH&S routine, non-routine, emergency and management system-related tasks. People performing these tasks should have the competence to perform them effectively and safely.
    o   Determine the competence criteria for each identified task or function. This must clearly include the required qualification, experience, skill and knowledge required to perform the task safely, efficiently and effectively.
    o   Ensure that personnel appointed on tasks associated with OH&S risks are competent, and meet the defined criteria of competence.
    o   Ensure that personnel are evaluated against the defined competency criteria at least once every year.
    o   Determine what additional training may be needed when a gap is found between the actual, and the defined, competence level.

2   Manager < > shall be responsible for preparing an annual OH&S training plan, as identified by the above need analysis process. In addition to the specific job-

related training, the plan must also include the following trainings which are relevant to all personnel:

o Emergency response training, muster points and head count system.

o Hazard identification and reporting process.

o The relationship between behaviour, attitude and safety.

o Consequences of departure from the laid down procedures and instructions.

o Fire-fighting and first aid.

o PPEs and general safety instructions that are applicable to all employees, such as wearing of seat belts, designated smoking areas, good dietary habits, basic hygiene, basic ergonomics, regular exercise and use of personal protective equipment.

3 Manager < > shall implement the annual training plan after receiving the budgetary approval from the finance department of SSI. Training plan must include all four categories of training, i.e., initial training, job specific training, general safety training and refresher training. It must be ensured that the training is given in a language, and at a level, that is fully understood by those receiving the training.

4 Manager < > shall ensure that training effectiveness is determined after each training, and where required, actions are taken to enhance the effectiveness of the training process. Training effectiveness will be determined by any one or more of the following methods:

o Taking feedback from trainees

o Taking feedback from the tutor

o Evaluating the results of the end of the course examination

o Receiving feedback on post training performance from the relevant supervisor.

5 Manager < > shall be responsible for maintaining records of training and education for all employees.

Appendix D: Sample Procedure for Training Competence and Awareness

Records that must be kept

- List of OH&S tasks and functions at SSI
- Record of competency criteria
- Record of training needs analysis
- Training plan
- Training conducted
- Training effectiveness.

APPENDIX E: DOCUMENTS REQUIRED BY OHSAS 18001

OHSAS 18001:2007 Clause ref.	Documents required by the standard
4.2	Occupational health and safety policy.
4.3.1	Procedure(s) for OH&S hazard identification, risk assessment and determination of controls.
4.3.1	Hazard and risk register.
4.3.2	Procedure(s) for legal, and other, requirements.
4.3.2	List of applicable legal, and other OH&S requirements, to which an organisation subscribes.
4.3.3	OH&S objectives, targets and programmes.
4.4.1	Documented roles, responsibilities and authorities for OH&S.
4.4.2	Procedure(s) for competence, training and awareness.
4.4.3	Procedure(s) for communication, participation and consultation.
4.4.4	Document that describes the scope and description of the main elements of OH&S and their interaction. Also includes, or gives reference, to procedures and other applicable documents.
4.4.5	Procedure(s) for control of documents.

4.4.6	Procedures for control of operations, activities, equipment and situations, where their absence could lead to harm, ill health or injury.
4.4.7	Procedure/plan for emergency preparedness and response.
4.5.1	Procedure(s) for monitoring and measurement.
4.5.2	Procedure(s) for periodic evaluation of compliance with applicable legal and other requirements.
4.5.3	Procedure(s) for incident investigation, non-conformity, corrective and preventive actions.
4.5.4	Procedure for control of records.
4.5.5	Procedure for internal OH&S audit.
Documents of external origin	These could be standards, laws, equipment manuals, and other reference documents originated by external organisations but applicable to the OH&S system of an organisation.

APPENDIX F: SAMPLE PROCEDURE FOR CRITICAL PRESSURE EQUIPMENT (CPE)

Purpose: To define a procedure for operation, maintenance and repair of critical pressure equipment operated by Safe & Sound Inc. (SSI).

Responsibilities:

- Manager <   > has the overall responsibility for implementation and maintenance of this procedure.
- A competent and authorised person shall be nominated (for each CPE), who shall have the overall responsibility for safety, operations and maintenance of the assigned CPE.
- Each CPE shall be operated and maintained only by operators who are competent, and authorised, for the specific CPE.

Scope:

- This procedure is applicable to all such pressure equipment which has the potential to cause a major safety incident, or poses a major safety risk.
- This shall include all vessels, piping, safety accessories and pressure accessories subjected to a maximum allowable pressure greater than 0.5 bar.
- Critical pressure equipment shall include steam boilers, autoclaves and storage vessels and cylinders for butane, hydrogen, propane and other compressed or liquefied flammable gases.
- Attached elements, such as flanges, supports, nozzles and couplings, are to be considered as integral components of CPE.

Procedure:

1 Manager <   > shall prepare an inventory of all critical pressure equipment (CPE) operated by SSI.

2   A competent person shall be nominated for each CPE. He/she shall be responsible for conducting a risk assessment for the assigned CPE. A hazard and operability study (HAZOP) shall be carried out for hazard identification, risk assessment and determination of controls for each CPE. The HAZOP must be revisited after every significant change or modification in the CPE, or after every three years (whichever is earlier).

3   The nominated competent person for each CPE must ensure that the CPE complies with the following regulatory requirements:
   o   ASME Boiler and Pressure Vessel Code or the European Pressure Equipment Directive.
   o   A detailed risk assessment based on HAZOP.
   o   All CPEs are fitted with at least one pressure relief valve.
   o   All safety devices protecting the CPE must be examined and tested at least once every year.
   o   Boilers must remain compliant with all requirements of British Standard 2790, European standard EN12953 and ASME standards.

4   The nominated competent person must ensure that each CPE meets the following operational and maintenance requirements:
   o   The equipment specific maintenance and operating procedure is available, understood and implemented for each CPE.
   o   Each CPE is marked/tagged to display specifications, such as manufacturer's name, serial number, year of manufacture, maximum and minimum design pressure and design temperature.
   o   Operators performing tasks on CPE must be competent and authorised.
   o   Safety controls and alarms must be automated.
   o   Boilers must have their water levels controlled automatically through a closed loop controlled system.

o The electronic flame failure detection device (for boilers) is inspected once every three months.

o Risk assessment must be done for all CPE, by a competent person, before carrying out any repair or modification.

o Ensure that the feed water for steam boilers is pre-processed, as defined in the boiler operating manual.

o Maintain the residual hardness of boiler water, as defined in the boiler operating manual.

o Ensure zero oxygen level is maintained in the boiler.

o Each CPE must have a plan for daily, weekly, monthly and annual maintenance/testing. The plan must also provide for testing and calibration of the safety equipment, alarms, pressure relief valves, trips and sensors installed on each CPE. The frequency of ultrasonic tests and magnetic particle inspection should also be included in the maintenance/testing plan.

o The implementation of the maintenance plan, and its results, must be recorded in a register. A separate and updated register, and a piping and instrumentation diagram (P&ID), shall be maintained for each CPE.

o The competent person for each CPE shall ensure that the competence of the operational and maintenance staff working on the CPE is annually checked against the defined criteria.

o Ensure that an audit of the CPE system is conducted once every year, and corrective actions taken where appropriate.

5 The competent person for each CPE shall ensure that all regulatory requirements are complied with at all times, and that all 'unsafe' conditions are reported. An 'unsafe condition' relating to pressure equipment is a condition that could result in an accident, leading to injury, death, or property damage. These could be conditions, such as faulty pressure components, malfunction of safety

devices, improper operation of the pressure equipment, unauthorised repair or alteration, loss of containment, etc.

6 The designated competent person for each CPE shall ensure that all maintenance and operations are carried out in accordance with the manufacturer supplied instructions, and all safety precautions and controls are fully implemented.

Records that must be kept

- HAZOP for each CPE
- Maintenance record for each CPE
- Testing and validation records for each CPE
- Updated register and P&ID for each CPE
- List of competent and authorised persons for each CPE
- List of competent and authorised operators designated for each CPE
- Record of unsafe conditions
- Record of calibration of instruments fitted on CPEs.

APPENDIX G: SAMPLE PROCEDURE FOR 'PERMIT TO WORK'

Purpose:

- To define a process for carrying out work using a 'permit to work' (PTW) certificate, in order to avoid serious incidents associated with potentially hazardous tasks.

- To ensure that Safe and Sound Inc. (SSI) complies with current general OH&S legislation, as well as specific regulation relating to 'work at height', 'confined spaces' and 'electricity at work'.

Responsibilities:

- Safety co-ordinator SSI has the overall responsibility to ensure maintenance, implementation and audit of this procedure.

- Permit issuer is the authorised person who issues the PTW, and is responsible for performing all functions stated in this procedure.

- Permit receiver is the person who understands all requirements, takes all the precautions and performs the tasks as defined in the PTW.

Scope: This procedure applies to all staff and contractors who undertake activities for, or on behalf of, SSI.

Procedure:

1   PTW is a written record that authorises specific work, at a specific work location, for a specific time period. PTWs are used as a 'control', to establish and maintain safe working conditions. They ensure that all foreseeable hazards have been considered, and that the appropriate precautions are defined and implemented. PTW may also be considered as an agreement between the issuer and the receiver that the applicable documents, conditions, precautions, limitations and responsibilities have been clearly understood.

2   PTW, being an operational control, must be identified in the risk assessment of a task. At SSI, it is mandatory to implement PTW for the following categories of tasks:
  o Working at heights (above two metres)
  o Working in confined spaces
  o Hot work (except in clearly designated areas, such as welding shop or engineering workshop)
  o Demolition or excavation
  o Process or pipeline, where there is a risk of exposure to hazardous materials
  o Work on high voltage electrical systems
  o Energy isolation, including working on electrical installations
  o Fire alarm isolation.

Each type of PTW defines the nature of hazards and the controls that must be in place for a specific task.

3   Departmental managers ensure that no work that falls in the above categories is undertaken in their departments, unless it complies with all requirements of PTW.

4   Permit issuer will ensure that a risk assessment has been conducted and a method statement prepared, before initiating a PTW.

5   In addition to the risk assessment and method statement, the permit issuer must undertake the following tasks:
  o Ensure that all hazards are clearly identified and explained to the permit receiver.
  o Ensure that the permit receiver, and their team, are competent to undertake the task.
  o Ensure that all precautions/controls are defined on the PTW, understood by the receiver and physically implemented. These instructions must include actions required to restore the area/equipment to a 'fit for use' or 'safe for work' status.
  o Ensure that lock out and tag out, or energy isolation steps, are clearly defined and implemented.
  o Allow the work to begin only after safety precautions have been fully implemented.

- o Ensure that the PTW specifies the exact nature of work, its location, and its start and finish timings.
- o Inspect the place where the work is to be undertaken, prior to signing of the PTW.
- o Once the work begins, check that all PTW precautions are being taken, and all controls are fully in place (at least once every day).
- o Ensure that the shift handover procedure (from one shift to another) is understood and implemented (where a shift change is involved).
- o Once the work is completed, permit issuer will re-inspect the area to ensure that the task has been completed satisfactorily, and the area or equipment has been restored to a safe working condition.
- o PTW issuer will retain one copy, give one copy to the PTW receiver, and send a completed PTW copy to the management representative after all tasks have been completed and the PTW has been closed.

6 The permit receiver has the following responsibilities:
- o To ensure that the method statement, risk assessment and PTW requirements, are fully understood by themselves and their team members.
- o To ensure that the work is done as defined in the PTW, and all defined precautions and controls are fully implemented.
- o To prominently display the PTW at the place of work.
- o To ensure that the persons who perform supporting roles, such as 'confined space' attendants or rescuers, those who undertake fire watch, or those who stay in touch with people working at heights, are competent to perform their assigned roles.
- o To constantly remain alert and ensure that all precautions and controls are fully implemented and effective.
- o To ensure that all guarding and safety systems are re-established and placed back at their original places before the energy isolations are removed.

- o To ensure that area or equipment is safely handed over to the user as defined in the PTW.
- o To ensure that a watch is kept for four hours after the hot work has been completed.

Records that must be kept

- One copy of the completed PTW will be kept by the management representative.
- One copy of PTW will be retained by the permit receiver.
- One copy of PTW will be retained by the permit issuer.
- Permit receiver will maintain the training and competence records of all persons who worked on a PTW task.
- Permit issuer will retain records of all risk assessment and method studies.
- Permit issuer will maintain records of all tests done. These may be tests, such as presence of gases in confined space, or tests done to determine the medical fitness of those who work on heights.

APPENDIX H: SAMPLE PROCEDURE FOR FORK-LIFT TRUCKS

Purpose:

- To define a procedure for fork-lift trucks (FLTs) used by Safe and Sound Inc. (SSI), so as to ensure safety in all aspects of their operations.

Responsibilities:

Supervisor FLTs is responsible for ensuring maintenance, implementation and audit of this procedure.

Procedure:

This procedure is applicable to all three fork-lift trucks operated by Safe and Sound Inc. (SSI).

Operations:

The following precautions/controls shall be exercised for operations involving all SSI fork-lift trucks:

- Ensure that all three SSI FLTs operate within their specified load limits, and follow operating instructions specified in their respective equipment manuals.
- An out of service, or 'unfit for use', fork-lift truck (FLT) will be clearly marked by a large sign, to avoid unintentional use.
- An FLT will not be used if its reversing horn is not in working order.
- FLTs shall only operate on their designated and marked routes. Pedestrian crossings on these routes shall be marked with bright yellow fluorescent paint.
- All FLTs will have over-speed horns to warn the driver if the speed limit is crossed. FLTs shall have a maximum speed limit of 5km/hour.
- The driver will always be wearing a seat belt when driving a FLT.

- FLT drivers will not use mobile phones under any circumstances while driving.

- Battery charging for FLTs must be done in a designated and well ventilated area which is at least three metres away from storage of any materials, goods or equipment. All battery chargers used by SSI should be fitted with overcharge protection.

- As all SSI FLTs use diesel, their refuelling must be done in the open air, with no materials or goods within three metres of the refuelling point.

- FLT keys are not to be left in the FLT when parked and not in use.

- When not carrying a weight, FLTs shall only move with forks in the down position. Signs of 'Both pedestrian and FLT to STOP when the distance is three metres and forks are in a raised position' must be prominently displayed along the FLT pathways.

Maintenance:

- Designated drivers shall inspect their FLTs every day, as per checklist displayed on each FLT.

- Any sparking FLT electrical motor shall be reported immediately, and the FLT should not be used until this has been fully repaired.

- Weekly, monthly and yearly FLT inspections shall be carried out as per manuals received from suppliers.

- Records of daily, weekly, monthly and yearly inspections shall be maintained.

Training and competence of drivers:

- Only equipment specific qualified (licensed) and authorised drivers shall be permitted to drive FLTs.

- Drivers should be reassessed and retrained for practical skill and ability every two years.

- Drivers should be physically fit to drive the FLT for full duty hours.

- Drivers should have no drug addiction, and must undergo an annual medical inspection, and also an annual test for eyesight.

- Driver training and medical records must be maintained.

Auditing:

The FLT supervisor, or any other person nominated by OH&S management representative, will carry out an audit of this procedure once every year, for compliance and effectiveness. Corrective actions shall be taken without undue delay. In case of an equipment-specific non-conformity, the concerned FLT will not be used until all corrective actions have been completed and found to be effective.

APPENDIX I: SAMPLE FORMAT FOR A
NON-CONFORMITY REPORT (NCR)

NCR No:	NCR Date:
Reference no of document against which this non-conformity is raised: Company procedure/OHSAS 18001/legal requirements/complaint from interested part/any other :	
Describe non-conformity:	
Signed: Date:	

Action taken to correct the non-conformity. Also describe mitigation actions taken (if any).   Signed:　　　　　　　　　Date:
Root cause (s)
Actions taken to eliminate root cause(s) to avoid recurrence :   Signed:　　　　　　　　　Date:

Appendix I: Sample Format for Non-Conformity Report (NCR)

Review of corrective actions for effectiveness :

Signed: Date:

APPENDIX J: SAMPLE FORMAT FOR OH&S RECORD CONTROL

Record Name	Record Number	Retention Period (years)	Maintained by	Location

APPENDIX K: SAMPLE INPUT REPORT FOR OH&S MANAGEMENT SYSTEM REVIEW

Input report for the management review to be conducted on 10.06.2012 by the top management of Safe & Sound Inc. (SSI).

1. Results and follow-up of internal OH&S audits, and evaluation of compliance with applicable legal and other requirements

The last complete system internal OH&S audit was carried out in October 2011. Additional audits were carried out for the following processes:

- Permit to work (April 2011)
- Emergency preparedness and response (May 2011).

Results and follow-up of complete system audit carried out in October 2011:

It was a four person-day audit carried out by trained internal OH&S auditors. Two non-conformities were identified, and their details are given below.

Non-conformity No.1: A minor cut received by a worker on 26/05/2011 while working on the cable assembly machine (CA 22) was not reported.

Root causes: (a) Insufficient worker training on incident reporting process. (b) Ineffective supervision, resulting in failure to comply with procedures.

Corrective actions taken: (a) Incident report raised and investigated. (b) Operator provided training on incident reporting process. (c) Training session also conducted for all other operators, to explain the incident reporting process. (d) All supervisors briefed to constantly remind operators on the need for reporting all incidents. (e) Incident reporting forms kept at prominent locations in all departments, and incident reporting procedure made a mandatory part of refresher training for all employees.

Non-conformity No.2: Annual medical examination of the workers conducted in June 2011 revealed that two operators working in the wire assembly area next to the boiler house had impaired hearing.

Root causes: (a) Noise survey not conducted in the plant for past four years. (b) Hazard identification and risk assessment process failed to identify noise risks for workers working in close proximity to the boiler house. (c) Lack of training/competence on the part of the risk assessment team. (d) Management failure to conduct noise surveys of the plant to identify high noise areas.

Corrective actions taken: (a) Hazard identification and risk assessment training process was reassessed and strengthened by the addition of two extra days of training. (b) Training effectiveness process was also revisited and a practical evaluation module added to evaluate participants' practical ability to conduct an effective risk assessment. (c) Noise survey was carried out for all locations of the plant. (d) Wearing of ear plugs and six monthly audiometric testing was introduced for all individuals working on, or near, high noise areas (above 80 decibels). (e) Annual noise survey of the plant was made a mandatory requirement.

'Permit to work' system audit conducted in April 2011

It was a process specific audit. The following non-conformity was identified in the PTW system.

Non-conformity: Hot Work procedure No. SSI-P-33 requires a fire watch to be carried out for four hours after the completion of hot work. The records show that the fire watch is currently being carried out for one hour only.

Root cause: (a) Inadequate knowledge of the current procedures. (b) Inadequate measuring and monitoring (c) Training programmes fail to cover the specific requirements stated in procedures and PTW.

Corrective actions taken: (a) Implementation of four hour fire watch was started with immediate effect. (b) All supervisors and workers involved in hot work were retrained on the requirements of PTW, as well as Procedure SSI-P-33. (c) Training programmes were revised, so that all individuals receive training on relevant procedures once every six months. (d) A system of weekly audit of PTWs was introduced.

Emergency preparedness and response audit in May 2011

It was also a process specific audit and its objective was to determine the effectiveness of the emergency preparedness and response system. The following non-conformity was identified:

Non-conformity: There was no evidence of regular testing of fire hydrants, fire alarms and emergency lights. Also, a number of employees had not received emergency response training, although they had already spent several months in the organisation.

Root cause: (a) Inadequate measurement, monitoring and inspection system (b) Lack of competence on the part of manager responsible for making equipment inspection plans. (c) Deficiency in training needs analysis and planning process.

Corrective actions taken: (a) All fire hydrants, alarms and emergency lights were inspected, and the rest of the emergency equipment was also checked, to ensure that they were working correctly. (b) All emergency equipment was listed and brought within the ambit of the measurement and testing programme. (c) The manager responsible for making the emergency equipment inspection plan was sent for specific training on emergency equipment inspection and planning procedures. (d) Emergency training for all new arrivals was made a mandatory requirement within the first week of their arrival. A check was carried out across the factory to ensure that all individuals had received the emergency training. Emergency training was provided to three persons who had been missed out.

Compliance with legal and other applicable requirements

The last annual verification of compliance with legal, and other requirements to which SSI subscribes, was conducted in March 2012. The results were as follows:

- SSI complies with all laws relating to occupational health, except the requirement of adequate noise control measures for locations where the noise level is above 85 decibels. OH&S objectives and targets have been established to meet this requirement.

- SSI complies with all safety laws, except that the two yearly Magnetic particle inspection for Boiler No.3 had not been done, and it was now overdue by three months. A non-conformity report has been raised and corrective actions are in process.

- SSI failed to submit a report to the concerned regulatory body for the lost time accident (LTA) that occurred in March 2012. A non-conformity report was raised, and all corrective actions have been taken to prevent recurrence of this incident in the future.

2. Results of participation and consultation

- Monthly departmental safety committee meetings are being held regularly. This ensures all personnel can bring out, and discuss, their OH&S-related issues and concerns. Corrective actions are taken on all issues raised and agreed by the safety committees.

- There was a suggestion to change the existing PTW procedure to include a mandatory requirement of a 'tool box' meeting before commencement of work on PTW. This suggestion was agreed upon and has now been included in the procedure.

- There were two complaints about lifting of heavy loads during the movement of cable drums from one department to another. This matter is under study and will need a management decision to change from manual lifting to using a conveyor belt.

- Workers identified the need for an emergency eyewash and shower machine to be installed at the entrance of production hall No.2. The suggestion was agreed upon and the machine has been installed.

- In the last six months, SSI received 25 OH&S suggestions from workers, while 18 new OH&S hazards were identified on a voluntary basis.

3. Communication from external interested parties

External communication took place with the regulatory body on non-reporting of LTAs. Corrective action has now been taken to prevent recurrence of delays in reporting.

4. OH&S performance of SSI

The following OH&S KPIs are being reported. They reflect the results of data collected over the past 12 months, and include both leading and lagging measures of OH&S performance.

OH&S KPIs	Results
Number of risk assessments completed	12
Number of OH&S equipment inspections carried out	6
Number of emergency drills conducted	2
Number of 'walk-around' or 'deep compliance' inspections completed	8
Number of 'behaviour safety' contacts made	16
Number of 'defensive driving' trainings conducted	2
Number of OH&S training and awareness sessions held	6

Number of near miss reports	24
Number of safety committee meetings held	26
Number of internal OH&S audits completed	3
Proactive monitoring of regulatory compliance	Being implemented
Number of lost time accidents (LTAs)	7
Number of restricted work cases (RWCs)	12
Number of medical treatment cases (MTCs)	14
Number of fatalities	Nil
Vehicle accidents	2 minor accidents.

5. Extent to which OH&S objectives and targets were met

SSI had established two OH&S objectives for 2012. These are:

a. Noise survey to be completed for all locations of SSI by June 2012. Where the existing noise level exceeds 85 decibels, engineering controls to be applied to bring the noise level to less than 80 decibels, by October 2012

Status: This objective has been 80% accomplished. Noise survey for all locations has been completed. Five high noise zones were identified. Isolation and noise suppression materials have been used to bring down the noise levels at three locations. Work is in progress on the last two locations and is expected to be completed by June 2012.

b. Reduce the number of medical treatment cases by 50% of its current level of 14 cases per year. Objective to be achieved by December 2012

Status: A management programme spread over six main areas of thrust, was prepared to accomplish this objective. These areas are (a) Improving training process for hazard identification and risk assessment. (b) Review of risk assessments, especially focused on departments where the majority of medical treatment cases originated last year. (c) Introducing 'behaviour safety' contacts that focus on behavioural issues linked with incidents. (d) Introducing safety trips and interlocks on all machines with a potential for injury or harm. (e) Ensuring full compliance to use of relevant personal protective equipment. (f) Each member of senior management to conduct walk-around audits (one per week) to identify areas of OH&S concerns, and take immediate actions to eliminate the causes.

6. Status of incident investigation and follow-up of corrective and preventive actions

Event	Progress
OH&S incidents investigated	6
Status	4 investigations fully completed and corrective actions implemented. 2 investigations still in progress and will be closed by 30 June 2012
Corrective actions initiated	14
Status	11 corrective actions completed and their effectiveness verified. These were initiated due to internal audits, as well as investigation of incidents. The remaining 3 corrective actions require top management decisions for grant of additional resources. This matter would be taken up

	and decided in the management review meeting to be held on 10.06.2012
Preventive actions and their status	2 preventive actions were initiated. (a) Installation of exhaust fans for reducing dust particle level in the packaging department and (b) installing barriers around fuel decanting area. Both preventive actions were successfully completed in April 2012

7. Follow up actions from previous reviews

The last management review was conducted on 12.10.2011. All 14 decisions of the last management review have been implemented.

8. Any changes that could impact upon an OH&S management system

Two changes have been introduced that can have a potential for new, or changed, occupational health and safety hazards. These are:

Construction of a new tank for storage of 1,000 gallons of diesel oil. SSI would need to obtain a licence from the government, before the storage activities can be initiated.

Two new cargo lifts have been installed, which require planning and implementation of maintenance, inspection, testing and certification programmes.

9. Recommendations for improvement

Two recommendations are being made for consideration by top management for continual improvement of the OH&S management system. These are:

1   The frequency of carrying out emergency drills should be increased from one drill per year, to two drills per year.

2   A reward system should be introduced to reward those 10 employees who report the highest number of hazards, and another 10 employees who give the most suggestions on hazard reduction and control.

Signed:

Management Representative (OH&S)

BIBLIOGRAPHIC NOTES

ISO19011:2011 Guidelines on quality and/or environmental management system auditing:
www.iso.org/iso/catalogue_detail?csnumber=50675

OHSAS 18001:2007, Occupational health and safety management system – Requirements:
www.ohsas-18001-occupational-health-and-safety.com/

ISO14001 Step by Step: A Practical Guide, Sadiq, N and Hayat, A, IT Governance Publishing (2011).

ITG RESOURCES

IT Governance Ltd sources, creates and delivers products and services to meet the real-world, evolving IT governance needs of today's organisations, directors, managers and practitioners.

The ITG website (*www.itgovernance.co.uk*) is the international one-stop-shop for corporate and IT governance information, advice, guidance, books, tools, training and consultancy.

www.itgovernance.co.uk/catalog/418 is the catalogue page on our website for resources connected with this pocket guide.

Other Websites

Books and tools published by IT Governance Publishing (ITGP) are available from all business booksellers and are also immediately available from the following websites:

www.itgovernance.co.uk/catalog/355 provides information and online purchasing facilities for every currently available book published by ITGP.

www.itgovernance.eu is our euro-denominated website which ships from Benelux and has a growing range of books in European languages other than English.

www.itgovernanceusa.com is a US$-based website that delivers the full range of IT Governance products to North America, and ships from within the continental US.

www.itgovernanceasia.com provides a selected range of ITGP products specifically for customers in South Asia.

www.27001.com is the IT Governance Ltd website that deals specifically with information security management, and ships from within the continental US.

Pocket Guides

For full details of the entire range of pocket guides, simply follow the links at *www.itgovernance.co.uk/publishing.aspx*.

Toolkits

ITG's unique range of toolkits includes the IT Governance Framework Toolkit, which contains all the tools and guidance that you will need in order to develop and implement an appropriate IT governance framework for your organisation. Full details can be found at *www.itgovernance.co.uk/ products/519*.

For a free paper on how to use the proprietary Calder-Moir IT Governance Framework, and for a free trial version of the toolkit, see *www.itgovernance.co.uk/calder_moir.aspx*.

There is also a wide range of toolkits to simplify implementation of management systems, such as an ISO/IEC 27001 ISMS or a BS25999 BCMS, and these can all be viewed and purchased online at: *www.itgovernance.co.uk/catalog/1*.

Best Practice Reports

ITG's range of Best Practice Reports is now at *www.itgovernance.co.uk/best-practice-reports.aspx*. These offer you essential, pertinent, expertly researched information on a number of key issues including Web 2.0 and Green IT.

Training and Consultancy

IT Governance also offers training and consultancy services across the entire spectrum of disciplines in the information governance arena. Details of training courses can be accessed at *www.itgovernance.co.uk/training.aspx* and descriptions of our consultancy services can be found at *www.itgovernance.co.uk/consulting.aspx*.

Newsletter

IT governance is one of the hottest topics in business today, not least because it is also the fastest moving, so what better way to keep up than by subscribing to ITG's free monthly newsletter *Sentinel*? It provides monthly updates and resources across the whole spectrum of IT governance subject matter, including risk management, information security, ITIL and IT service management, project governance, compliance and so much more. Subscribe for your free copy at: *www.itgovernance.co.uk/newsletter.aspx*.

Lightning Source UK Ltd.
Milton Keynes UK
UKOW05f0747240916

283706UK00015B/450/P